TIME'S REFUGEE

TIME'S REFUGEE

Poems

FREDERICK FEIRSTEIN

Story Line Press | *Pasadena, CA*

Time's Refugee
Copyright © 2021 by Frederick Feirstein
All Rights Reserved

ISBN 978-1-58654-062-3 (tradepaper)
       978-1-58654-116-3 (casebound)

The National Endowment for the Arts, the Los Angeles County Arts Commission, the Ahmanson Foundation, the Dwight Stuart Youth Fund, the Max Factor Family Foundation, the Pasadena Tournament of Roses Foundation, the Pasadena Arts & Culture Commission and the City of Pasadena Cultural Affairs Division, the City of Los Angeles Department of Cultural Affairs, the Audrey & Sydney Irmas Charitable Foundation, the Kinder Morgan Foundation, the Meta & George Rosenberg Foundation, the Allergan Foundation, the Riordan Foundation, Amazon Literary Partnership, and the Mara W. Breech Foundation partially support Red Hen Press.

First Edition
Published by Story Line Press
an imprint of Red Hen Press
www.redhen.org

Acknowledgments

Poems in this volume first appeared in *American Arts Quarterly, Hudson Review, Kenyon Review, Life & Legends, Ontario Review, Pivot, Poetry, Ploughshares, Quarterly Review of Literature, Salmagundi,* and *Trinacria.*

For Linda

CONTENTS

Time must have a stop.
—Aldous Huxley

The young become adults.
The adults become elders.
The elders become spirits.
—Ifeanyi Menkiti

GRAVEDONA

Lost in Gravedona without a map,
You ask directions in handicap
Italian of a stout old woman.
She laughs "Stop struggling, come in,
And whilst I think them out, I'll make us tea
And, if you don't mind, have a chat with me,
For I'm half-Welsh, half-Genovese."
Her father built this house, planted trees
"That will outlive this century. I'll bore
You maybe nattering about the war.
I need to take the rust off of me tongue,
Living as I do among young
People who take up German. Whoosh, it makes me boil,
Me who dieted on castor oil.
So," she smacks her stomach, "me bag is packed,
Time's refugee, ready to be attacked."

She waddles to the kitchen to make tea.
You ease into her affability,
Scanning her knickknacks, cheap paperbacks,
Miniature Union Jacks,
Photos of The Pieta, her son;
No, her husband, arms crossed with a gun,
"That's right, like me he was a Partisan
Hid in these hills. They tortured him, poor man,
When a spy, born in this town, gave him up.
She pours the tea, then hot milk in my cup.
She spots the admiration in my eyes.
"Pettiness survives, heroism dies.
Isn't that so in The States?
                              "Sure,
We've lost our confidence with our naiveté.

We've given up what Hitler couldn't take.
Grinning, she slices a home-baked cake.
During the war, fat me was the head
Of The Resistance here. I baked the bread,
I bought the books . . . Yes, in Dongo, I
Helped capture Mussolini. Heels to sky
He hung, a creature out of Dante's Hell.
"I'll die with many stories I could tell.
Unlike you, young people here don't care
About the blood and terror in the square
They drink their coffee in. It's only we
Who are afflicted with this history:
Hitler, Goebbels, Goering—facts and names,
Heroes now in children's video games.
Just Once Upon A Time And Long Ago."
Her eyes begin to close. It's time to go.
"Tea finished already? You'll want your map.
I've traced it. Seems I can't resist me nap,
Journeying to a better world I knew.
You've not too far to go. Here's luck to you."
She clicks her cup against my empty cup.
"Hail and farewell," she grins, "and bottoms up."

FRIENDS

We lay on the floor, the sun shining
On our quaint and innocent bodies.
Around us, our old friends the tiger
And the dependent worm,
The affectionate spaniel, gazing at us from crossed paws:
Millennia of experimentation with nerve and blood cell.
Somewhere, a solitary man,
Terrified of his children's touch,
His prehensile squint a coin-slot,
Abstractly plots our downfall.
Mixing chemicals no leukocyte has ever known,
He will destroy plant and animal,
Anything not lifeless and marketable,
Anything historical and therefore helpless.
And still the planets will turn
And the galaxies will wander
Inexorably toward their final doom.
So, when I touch you with wonder and grief
I am being nothing but political.

STRESA

Since you read Stendhal, Flaubert, De Musset,
Isola Bella seemed a hazy dream:
Ramparts of gardens rising out of water,
Water nymphs stunned into statuary,
Grottos where walls of pebbles and mortar
Formed sea shells and sea creatures,
Rooms with mandolins and *violas d'amores*,
Balustrades where assignations were made
With a nod, a wink, the snap of a fan.

All was true enough, as the German guide
Declaims in gutturals: This was the conference room
Of Ramsay MacDonald and Mussolini.
Here Napoleon slept and stepped outside
To sniff dahlias and rhododendrons.
There in that maze of midget hedges
Peacocks and cardinals mixed, flaunting their plumage.
History, like this baroque estate
Was mere fantasy: Nazis and Popes,
Servants and lizards, water nymphs and devils,
As in the puppet theater before the grottos
Where a procession of townspeople
Display the Deadly Sins that shaped their faces.

You unfold the Herald Tribune under your arm
And stare at the photo:
"Russian Grandchildren Delve Into History."
A woman in a babushka and flowered frock
Weeps over a skull she cradles in her hands.
*"Plucked from a mass grave dug in Stalin's terror,
Or in World War II."* The guide squints as if she held
A relic, then turns back to joke

About a statue of, "A Chinaman
Two centuries old, *forse,* Mao Tse-tung."

The crowd laughs as if they've lived forever
And moves on to the outdoor amphitheater,
Black and gray in the sunlight, its gardens
Cemeterial, its statuary
Looking past Stresa where Mussolini fled
And the crowd, mindful of history, caught him
By the heels in Dongo, till he swung
Like the pendulum of a Borromean clock.

THE POND

Nature is never wrong, the lilies say,
Simply alive in the pond, life goes on,
Despite carnivorous violence, firestorms.
We are porcelain quiet. Sit on this bench
Listen to The Baroque Ensemble play
Music composed during The French
Revolution; cherish the bees
Closed in our petals, close your eyes,
Close them, close yourself in these harmonies.
All civilizations die.

TRUMMELBACH

A typically Swiss German, typically neat
Valley of chocolate houses with red
Raspberry flowerboxes and toy trains,
And cable cars and Heidi and Julie Andrews
Dancing among the clean sheep of the vast
Almighty mountain peaks, and almost audible
Yodeling and *glockenspieling* and *lieder*
Singing and church bells ringing: *Peace*
For Chrissakes, peace. In this
Typically Swiss German, typically neat
Valley, you stand before Trummelbach,
Meaning *Streams Like Drums,* before
Slopes covered with wildflowers and harp string grass,
Beneath cloud-untrammeled, serenely blue sky.
Trummelbach. The name resonates
With romantic pomposity as you ascend
The mountain's rectum in a steep dark
Cable car. *Trummelbach,* into whose bowels
The Munch, Eiger, and Jungfrau pour
Twenty thousand tons of glacial detritus per year
Trummelbach, where all boundaries are broken,
The ancient hidden shit-world of Europe,
Hitler's kingdom, the fury behind the borders
Of the Swiss dour face. *Trummelbach,*
The burst ethnic borders of Yugoslavia,
Of the fake Russian Empire: Georgia.
Armenia, Moldavia, Azerbaijan.
Trummelbach, Trummelbach, Streams Like Drums.
You walk from one bellowing waterfall,
Small Niagaras, to another, slipping, clutching the guard rail,
Staring in terror and awe, *Che Bella,*
Grand Merveilleux, Seig Heil!—Trummelbach.

EDGE

To set aside rage
And sit quietly at the water's edge
At the edge of yourself
And go past it
And live in the body of the duck
And the water lily
And the crumbs of your own gift of bread

DISNEY ON PARADE

Wheeling down Main Street in technicolor light
Are Disney's heroes, our mythology,
A comfort in the middle of the night.

Mickey Mouse, Minnie, Uncle Donald help.
The children of America are sick
Of war, cultural suicide, and greed.
Snow White, Bambi, Lady and the Tramp,
It's midnight now, help us in our hour of need.

You helped us with the witch's oven and
Her poisoned mushrooms. Goofy, Pluto please.
Those childhood traumas were much worse than these.
Teach us to be courageous and naïve.

FAIRYTALES

Storytellers know what scholars learn:
That we in time, because of time, must burn,
And to the womb of Death we must return.

Fairytales tell us what we can't forget:
That we are always children, to expect
The witches' woods of trauma and neglect.

In almost every fairytale we've ever heard
We children can't be seen, can't say a word
And know our Fate must always be absurd.

For instance, when the father suffers grief,
He sends us children to our stepmom's double
Who puts us on a cross or *bas relief.*

Our task, then, is to be resurrected
By challenging the unexpected,
To re-appear the fractally perfected.

Hansel and Gretel, Snow White are the best
To learn from, learn never to trust or rest
—The poorest of us and the wealthiest.
When we toast Life, remember we're Death's guest.

SNOW WHITE

Her face is now a zero of despair
Over aging, money, the fatality
Of menopause, sexual schemers . . .
She lifts a wisp of gray hair
And tries to grin, "Bring me no more dreamers."

Now is her final chance to meet The Prince.
"My inner wars are over, I need *peace,*
Not the poison of my mother's 'No!'
I've wakened to the dreaded Five Oh!

"Hurry, Prince, soon I will be bleeding.
Time brings one down incalculably slow.
My heartbeat's rapid, terrified of giving.
Like hers, hers, hers!
Hurry, Prince, I'm so tired of living."

THE PRINCE

In this fairytale of rescue we know well,
No one talks of The Prince and what he's giving
—His confidence, his courage, and his hope

Despite his journeys through his inner hells
—His fire-breathing Sis who couldn't cope
With masculinity and independent living

—Like Pop who would debase his youthful hope:
"Your sacrifice will make your sister well.
Watch me with Mom who's never unforgiving."

So here's Snow White, apparently not living.
Behind her glass, she doesn't look too well.
Yet The Prince still has the innocence to hope

He can resuscitate her with this kiss he's giving.
Warmed by the fire in her inner hell,
He doesn't hear her cackle, "Your breath's smoke,"

Or see the Mother Witch inside her unforgiving,
Or the Victim shouting in the mirror, "I can't cope!
This Prince here thinks I'm actually living?

"He doesn't know I'm happiest with dopes,
My seven ex-s with their dwarfish giving:
I'm happiest, poor Prince, when I'm not feeling well,

"For I was fed red apples plucked from Hell.
I can't digest your antidote of giving:
Your confidence, your courage, and your hope!"

The Prince thus lonely, maddened, learns to cope.
And, though he doesn't feel or look too well,
To stay alive he constantly keeps giving
While over him she knots a zero-rope.

GRETEL'S MOM

I ran out of to the house
The world said Boo
I ran back to the house
My mother said I
I ran out of the house
The world said Die
I ran back to the house
My mother said Why
I ran out of the house
The world said Who
I ran back to the house
My mother said Lie
I ran out of the house
The world said Dread
I ran back to the house
My mother was dead

HANSEL AND GRETEL

Hansel and Gretel, almost starving, fed
On sacramental pumpernickel bread,
Were led into a petrifying wood.
They played with animated animals
As children or the persecuted do,
Surviving but emaciated, till
They came upon a crippled witch's house,
Made of cakes and honeyed bread and candied vines.
They ravished them until the witch came out
On crutches, she said, "From the First World War."
Her mouth was black, her eyes were Nazi red.
"I'll fatten you on lies," she bluntly said,
"Which you will swallow, knowing you've no choice."
Then led them in, and music stirred their souls.
Vases were full of roses, lilacs, ferns.
On tables were dark chocolates for their hearts.
And, though she didn't say they were, sweetbreads
She plucked from other children's guts.

They ate so fast, they quickly fell asleep.
A crescent moon gave way to Aryan sun.
She lifted Hansel, lay him in a cage
And, while he rubbed his head in disbelief,
She ordered Gretel, "Fatten him on meat,
And rice and cheese, *sacher torts,* and pies.
This mixture will make all of him taste nice:
His hands, his feet, his eyeballs, and his ears.
I'll sing for you and put to sleep your fears."
Her lullaby entranced Gretel to feed
Hansel who ate till his small stomach swelled.

But he secreted a long chicken bone
Because he knew all witches are compelled
To re-enact their evil ways each day.
He knew that in his stepmom's witch's house.
So when she'd pinch to see if he was plump,
He's stick the bone out like a soldier's stump.
Fed up at last, the witch lit the waiting oven
And ordered Gretel to creep in and test
To see if it was getting Auschwitz-hot.
Gretel delayed. "Fatwa!" the witch exclaimed
And stuck her head in, stupid in her vice.
Gretel shoved her, bolted the oven door:
"Now howl, Mother. *We* will taste what's 'nice.'"
Strong as a Sabra, she unlocked the cage
And led her brother out, uneaten, free.
They scooped up all the witch's cakes
And brought them home. Poppa was overjoyed.
The witch he married, Tyranny, was dead.
They danced and sang and on the future fed.

THE WITCH

In Freud's Vienna no one could believe
The children they molested there could feel,
Although from fairytales they did expect
The Witch to heat up children for a meal.

What parents do, what friends of parents do,
What supers, teachers, clergy fix, explore,
Repeats itself in self-deception, war.
You know this as a persecuted Jew.

Read your memories Time makes ideal.
The text is there in metaphors and dreams,
In plays, poetry, even business schemes,
In masquerades of prayers against The Real.

Our lives were spent at two, three, four,
Watching a movie X-rated, humming
The sound track at our parents' door
—We sometimes hear it when we're coming.

For years, decades you repeat the trauma
In myth, the fairytale of World War II;
You bring your past into the drama,
Dreaming you're gathering gold teeth, brown shoes.

LITTLE RED RIDING HOOD'S BREAKDOWN

Little Red Riding Hood, traumatized,
—Her mind a blank till she was sixty-three,
Grandma's age, when she was analyzed
And freed from masochistic misery

That wrecked her adult life. Although her smile
Was charming, her conscious actions kind.
Her maddening innocence managed to beguile
Sadistic men who'd help her lose her mind.

She asked to be devoured where she stood,
Offering her custard, hungry for the belief
That the wolf was Grandma, that she should
Be gullible and offer herself to die.

When we're molested at an early age,
Before our consciousness absorbs the fact
And depression strikes with repressed rage,
We suffer nightmares we must re-enact.

So pre-pubescent Little Red Riding Hood
Endured a wolf *earlier* than her tale,
A stranger in the flower-sprinkled wood
Whom she enticed, succumbed to. Later, pale,

With deep black eyes, sexually dressed in red,
Indulged by Ma as she would murderous men,
She sent the second wolf to Grandma's bed
Where he would wolf her down from feet to head.

WOLF PHILOSOPHY

I have the nature of a wolf which means
I'm just rambunctious. I don't mean harm.
I'm constitutionally made of guile.
I mean to eat you; therefore, when I smile
That doesn't make me evil, just a wolf
Who uses what in business is called "a pitch."
I'm not malicious like The Witch
Who has alternatives, like being nice.
I'm like the cat who's programmed to eat mice.

MYTHS

Groping for consolation in The Final Stage
So we'll seem less crazy for our childrens' sake,
We make our re-enactments *Tragedies*
Where we're heroic, though we know we're fake.

Or, atheists start singing of The Soul
Like Yeats, that loony who we'd have ridiculed
When younger, braver, realer. Who'd believe
We'd harmonize in his strange singing school?

But, better, there's real comedy to tell
If we can find the insight and the will
To tease ourselves into those tiny hells
Where we, chronically children, all fall ill.

When he was lucid, Jung described the scenes
Where we're compelled to re-enact dark myths
That we can glimpse in fairytales and dreams,
As when he dreamed himself Christ The Fish.

Freud found his myth in self-analysis
Where Orpheus, ne Oedipus, he led
Us lost boys, naked to our souls' abyss
—To see in flashbacks what we missed in bed.

So ask yourselves, what myth became your Fate,
What traumas drew you in to play what part,
What self-deceptions, and what hypnoid states
Determined what exactly broke your heart.

REAL COMEDY

You contemplate a European lake
Where picnickers enact a comedy
Of Aryan romance: an ingénue
Eludes a subtle pass a soldier makes.

A chunky salesman, drunk and oniony,
Gooses a widow as she's dishing stew.
You're spooning chocolate mousse or German cake
Enjoying temporary sanity.

You see the agony awaiting you:
The nightmare when the 20th Century wakes
Amidst the litter of the bourgeoisie,
You see this as an analyst and Jew.

It doesn't matter what discoveries you make
About the psyche and its history.
Time and the world will have its way with you.
Yet for a moment, the future is opaque.

You're laughing with your living family.
The day is sunny and the lake is blue.

TWENTIETH CENTURY

A winter evening under a John Sloan El.
Fedoras tilt in unison against the wind.
The pink neon lights of a Polish bar
Invite Grandpa in, while my son
Does pushups on the rug, and I chin
In my mother's kitchen, and my uncle
Argues he could beat Willie Pep
If Grandpa would let him turn pro. I burn
In his disappointment sixty years ago.
Now Grandpa comes brawling into the street
And, arm-weary, staggers home on schnapps
And sits me down to watch Sugar Ray dance
Till he turns into *Counting Crows,* and my son
In my uncle's pecks flexes in the window
Where stenos in thin coats huddle against the snow.
One of them my mother, seeing my unborn face
In a taxi, hails it and rushes home.

TO MY YOUNGER SELF

The past is like a library after dark
Where we sit on the steps trading stories
With characters we imagined ourselves to be.
Neighbors in clothing from our childhood stroll by,
Unmolested, nodding at us, benevolently.
One with your father's face tips his fedora.
You lower your eyes in shame. I look back.
Someone is sitting at a long table,
Reading in the moonlight . . . I must look startled.
He holds a forefinger to his lips
As if it is a candle for the dead.
You tap me on the shoulder and I turn back.
The street is dangerously empty
Except for a newsstand lit yellow,
Where your mother in a nightgown
Showing beneath her blue coat buys the *Times,*
A pack of *Kools* and, eyeing us, lights one.
You race to her, turn a corner. Goodbye.
I'm frightened, as if I am a foreigner
In a city under siege. Yet I know
It is still mid-century. Underground
Are only subways carrying boisterous
Party-goers or somber family men
Working the night shift or harmless bookies
Respectful of the No Parking signs.
I walk to where the newsstand, shut,
Advertises brand names I'd forgotten.
I shove my hands into my pockets and whistle
A song we danced to when we were young.
I walk on for blocks, until I smell
Smoke from the burning borough of the Bronx.

RE-READING

When we re-read the story of our lives,
The genre changes with the characters
And what, for instance, seemed a bawdy comedy
Becomes, with consequences, tragedy,
And our best qualities become our worst.
So bravery, for instance, and tenacity
Become impulsiveness, rigidity . . .
Often re-reading is like reading Braille
When we're not blind—we can see it makes no sense
Any more than a sleepwalker's dream,
Our arms outstretched with meaning, till Time wakes us
To what is strangely present, dangerous.
And so in many colors, tongues we pray,
God have mercy on us, God have mercy on us.

HOME MOVIES

"Come home, come home," the failure family said,
"Where everyone is ailing or depressed.
We have washed your food, we have made your bed.
Come into the darkness and get undressed."

Have you ever watched an animal brought down
Step by tired step, traumatized and dazed?
I used to tap dance though my all-night town
Like Fred Astaire, debonair and unfazed

By the Depression that brought others low,
Squabbling around our wooden kitchen table.
I danced on my imagination's marble, slow,
While on the set Cain was murdering Abel.

"Come home," said Envy with its grin and wink,
"You are no different from the rest of us."
"Oh no, I feel so passionate and think,
Therefore I am." "Damn," they said, "don't cuss,"

And kept on muttering hypnotically
How my strength was self-made and, therefore, weak,
Until they robbed me of my energy
Until I joined them cheek to cheek.

"I'm home, I've failed, I'm sick, depressed.
I'm nothing but a creature of your time,
Fleeing pogroms, a little Russian Jew,
A Chaplin shrugging, 'Living is a crime?'"

In our central myth, Dorothy tries to strive
Toward selfhood in a country green as money,
But learns she's merely dreaming to survive,
Tricked by the Wizard, just her Aunt Bee's "Honey."

"Darn, if it isn't true," says Fred Astaire
"There's no place like home, there's no place like home."
He's watching Judy Garland climb a stair
Made of marble, slick as cemetery stone.

When small I thought my family film stars too,
Not as they were, I came to realize—as I dreamed.
My family were assimilated Jews,
Who dropped dead when their own ghosts schemed.

"Come home," like cozy families everywhere,
Hiding from cyclones in the gentile West,
Cossacks of wind that fractured Fred Astaire
And Judy Garland who came home to rest.

PARENTS

Night after night, as Age walks through my rooms,
Like a clown waddling on stilts of bones,
I smell your bodies, though you're bodiless,
And understand how easily you were doomed
By business failures, panics, medical mistakes
Which I have suffered for my soul's sake,
And need you in this dark and spooky Age
—As nights when you'd go out like candlelight,
Leaving the smoke of your pipe and cigarette,
Your perfume and your after-shave cologne.

FATHER AND SON

Finally I've learned forgiveness at this age,
For your mistakes that crippled me,
Which I've repeated. I have seen far worse.
You made them out of ignorance, not choice.

The rage I had, the wisdom that I lacked
Amaze me now, as if a page
That I was reading suddenly caught fire
And images of you tumbled from the smoke,
Words you mumbled when you were very tired,

Dying, your hand in mine, that long last night
Both knowing you had lost all breath to fight.
"It's late," you said, "I don't want you to go.
But you have to leave me." So I sighed

And, like a child in winter, buttoned up my coat.
"I love you," we said simultaneously.
"Kiss your son for me" who then was four months old.
The next day you were found unsaveable and cold.

So if I try to save you on this page
And if you try to save me from your realm,
Eons away, distances so vast
It seems a microscopic stage our past

Of father and son struggling through myth
Which we enacted witlessly and sick,
Dumb, irreconcilable, compelled
To make this seeming paradise a hell

In which we sleptwalked like the shade you are,
The shadow of a man I hoped to be.
Why were we burdened, little you and me
Or, as you often said, "How can this be?"

ACUPUNCTURE AND MOZART

Calmed at my heart's meridian, I spin
Mozart to pirouette on his royal blue disc.
His strings are dainty and his woodwinds brisk.
His keyboard strokes sound quaintly feminine.

Mozart's metronome, invisible and mute,
Leads me to find my mother with my *chi:*
Unblocked, pure kinesthetic memory
Urged on by oboes, violins and flutes—

All fingers trilling. Now a bow drawn slow-
Ly across the body of a cello
Quiets the strings to weep *adagio.*
The cello double stops and the winds gasp, Oh!

Now a solo, grieving violin
Sings on an E-string how it can't take death.
I watch my mother's Quan Yin hold her breath.
It's time again for mourning to begin.

VASE

Suddenly it's a hundred years ago
Or more, and you and Dad are in a store
On Madison or Park or five blocks
From home on East Broadway,
Or you're alone in your white gloves and swank hat
With all your secretarial savings in a purse
—And suddenly you see this Chinese vase
Lit up as it is on my shelf:
With mother and child on four sides, her gown
Green, a table before them trans-parent,
A vase of paint brushes, a pot of incense,
Five hundred or five thousand years old
Cherry blossoms in a cylindrical vase,
Vase within vase, time within time.

She guides the boy's hand to write.
Mandarin? Cantonese? Certainly not
Yiddish with its Chinese-looking letters,
Backwards writings she could not read
In the shtetl where no father could guide her hand,
But here instead, stitching clothes in a cleaning store
In the South Bronx, the Iron Curtain between them. What?
A mere century or so ago. The light dims as it must.
Another day is passing tick tock tick tock.
I pick up the telephone, my landline,
And call underground as once she fled
Through the Jewish Underground
—From Kamenitz Podolsk to Rotterdam
At eleven, ten years before she became snazzy,
Chic, in some store somewhere, gone
Like a brushstroke.
But alive, the cuneiform says. When?

from CHAUCER'S GENERAL PROLOGUE: A RE-CREATION

In gypsy April, when rambunctious showers
Rush life into the slender roots of flowers
And tickle every vein until the season
Is wriggling like a slut without a reason
But to entice the strolling passerby
To kiss his fingers at the brightening sky;
When robins fly with earthworms in their beaks
And Zephyrus with his bagpipe player's cheeks
Resuscitates the earth with barley breath,
Saving the skinny flocks again from Death;
And when the sun is pandering to youth,
Opening up the season's kissing booth
For a new pair of lovers red and swollen
Trading long rolls of tickets they had stolen,
And also for a pair of hummingbirds
Who match their music to the lovers' words;
It's in this gypsy April that the people,
Yearning to wrap their arms around a steeple
Will wrap their legs around a horse instead
And stuff their pockets full of cheese and bread
And tie their kerchiefs into traveling bags
And turn the heads of thoroughbreds and nags
To where the bell of Canterbury chimes
For martyred Thomas Becket who in times of illness
They had sought with only prayers
And a couple of the Pardoners holy wares . . .

It happened this season at the Tabard,
A hostelry in Southwerk where I blabbered
To the Host filling my goblet up with wine
About my love for Thomas Becket's shrine,
That a group of pilgrims, twenty-nine in all,

Who met by chance at Southwerk's flowered mall,
Tugged at the Host for beds to stay the night.
The Host could plainly see that some were tight.
But most were truly pious folk, so he
Allowed the drunks to steal the upstairs key . . .

There came my lady nun, the PRIORESS
She made you want to kneel down and confess.
Her smile was coy, was slower than a cat's.
Her strongest oaths were "Goodness me!" and "Rats!"
Her name was Madame Eglantine, and she
Could sing the service most exquisitely.
In choir she would always take the lead,
Her tongue a fluttering leaf, her nose a reed.
At table she was careful as a bird.
When chewing she refused to say a word.
She'd never let a morsel touch her lip
And never stain her fingers when she'd dip.
Oh, she would dab her upper lip so clean
That smudges on her cup were never seen.
She sometimes seemed a lady of the court,
Ready to join in intrigue or in sport.
For animals she had such tender care
That she'd kneel weeping if she saw a hare
Caught in a trap, wriggling and bleeding.
She had an Irish hound that she was feeding
—Secretly, with roasted meat and bread.
She loved to scratch its belly, kiss its head—
Although it was forbidden by her order.
"These rules!" she said, they sometimes simply bored her.
Her eyes were grey, her nose was finely shaped.
Her veil was pleated properly and draped

About a high-cheeked, but a seal-shaped head.
Her tiny mouth was very soft and red.
Her cloak was tailored well and I could see
That on her wrist she wore a rosary.
The larger beads were green and from them spun
A brooch as shiny as the re-born sun
And on it was inscribed a crowned "A"
And after *Amor vincit omnia* . . .

There was a FRIAR, sprightly, wanton, merry,
A begging Friar with a breath of sherry.
None was a better flatterer or flirt
Among the men who wore the hairy shirt.
And yet he was a decent soul; he wed
Husbands to every slut who crossed his bed.
This Friar was a pillar of his order,
Although he seemed to be a traveling boarder
Of Franklins, if their suppers made him belch.
His father was an Arab, mother Welsh
(Or so he told the widows whom he cuddled)
And when he heard confession, if you muddled
The details of your sins or left some out,
He wasn't petty—if you gave him stout
And venison or mallets or a kiss,
And then he'd sit with you and reminisce
About these details and give absolution
With water or your vinegar solution.
His hood was stuffed with rhinestone pins and knives
That served as gifts for penitential wives
Who turned their husbands' pockets inside out
In order to be touched by this devout
Begging Friar, this saint—Francis's ghost,

This rock, this rod, this holy hitching post!
He didn't wear a scholar's threadbare cape.
His robe was double-breasted and its shape
Was modeled on his monastery's bell.
He wore a bracelet strung with cockleshell.
His toenails like his fingernails were black
And when he laughed he had a smoker's hack.
At puberty, he said, he learned to lisp
Although his t's and d's were very crisp.
He was precise in business and in prayer.
He rode to stimulate him a young mare.
He loved her best, he said, when she upreared . . .

There was a MERCHANT with a forked brown beard,
A brown mustache, a matching beaver hat
And, as if posing for a brush, he sat
Rigid on his horse, his reins smartly slack.
His boots were polished to a wet crow's black.
His fingernails were filed, his nose hairs clipped.
His coat was muted tapestry, some script
—A corny Latin phrase—adorned his hem.
Each pinky bore an oriental gem.
His words were few, as if inscribed in gold:
What men he bought, what markets he controlled.
He was impassioned by a sole ideal:
"Protect the seas from buccaneers who steal
The wool from ships, those helpless lambs that sail
Between the cities of . . . Here's where I fail.
I am so ignorant of money that
I never will afford a sable hat."
This worthy man so well-employed his brain
That every thought was of financial gain.

Such dignity, such reverence he had
For what he could subtract, divide, or add.
He was a slugger in the business game.
But truthfully I can't recall his name . . .

The FRANKLIN'S beard was white, his face was red.
He dunked in red wine tufts of barley bread
For breakfast, then on roasted goose he'd munch
—Tidbits of meat in crackling skin—till lunch.
There was no flesh-bound pleasure he would shun,
For he was Epicurus's own son.
When he would host you, there was no restraint.
His fields were yours, Julian was his saint.
His bread and ale were always of the best.
For company, his fowls were always dressed.
His house was always stocked with baked meat pies
Stuffed with sirloin chunks from the fair's first prize,
And mackerels, lobsters, rainbow trout, and clams,
And molds of jelly from the hooves of lambs.
He changed his menu when God changed the season.
His feasting, therefore, always followed reason.
Many a partridge fattened in his coop.
His fish pond could be heated into soup.
His cook was fired if his sauce was flat
Or if his knives were duller than a gnat.
And when the county justices would meet,
He banged the gavel and he held a seat
In Parliament—he'd nibble nuts and dates
While others stuffed themselves with dull debates.

There came what you might call the constant WIFE.
She lived outside of Bath, and all her life

She toiled at making cloth till merchants paid
More for her goods than goods the Flemish made.
If someone stole her place in line when she
Filled the poor box, poof went her charity,
Her wrath resounding like an organ note.
She had less patience than a rutting goat.
Her hose was silk, red as a harlot's tongue.
Her shoes were new and felt as soft as dung.
Her face was round and splotched red as a berry.
She left five husbands at the cemetery.
When she was single, she hit all the haystacks, but
She felt until she married in a rut.
This pious woman traveled to Bologne
To cleanse herself and also to Cologne.
Five times she traveled to the Holy Land
And knew the Roman catacombs first-hand.
She was adept at wandering by the way.
She was gap-toothed and when she tried to say
"Sexy," for instance, you could see her tongue.
As her horse ambled, so her buttocks swung.
She called her fat hips "mermaid's dulcimers."
Her tiny feet clattered with silver spurs.
She wore a wimple and a velvet hat
That was as wide and blacker than a bat.
She talked incessantly, knew all the tricks
Of love, that is, "my rose-garden of pricks . . ."

The MILLER had a head and fist of rock.
With either he could break a butcher's block.
His biceps were an old tree's twisted roots.
His teeth were bigger than the nails of boots.
He was broad-shouldered with a stunted neck.

He'd cripple you if you said "Hell" for "Heck."
His mustache was the color of a fox,
The nose above was stolen from an ox.
Upon the very tip he had
A mole and from it grew a myriad
Of hairs as red as bristles of a sow.
His lips and tongue were stolen from a cow:
His voice was loud, roared at his ribald tales
All full of bulls who pissed in milkmaids' pails.
He was adept at stealing corn and grain
While looking at you and talking plain.
He played bagpipe with a cockeyed frown
And with it he would lead us out of town . . .

SPRING MUSIC

Philip, Billy, Roger, Bob, and Ted
Won't see this spring, or any other season.
There's not one pair of eyes among the dead.
Spring's rhythmical and rhymed, devoid of reason.
The birds are trilling bits of Bach and Brahms.
The vines are improvising drafts of psalms.
The seemingly senescent cherry trees
Open fresh flowers, pink and white and red
For our gardener listening, eyes closed, on his knees
As if they're whole notes rising from the dead.
The sky insists it's innocently blue,
That nothing happened; not, my friends, to you.

OTHERS

There is a timeless world in which they live,
In which old wounds are healed, right paths are taken,
In which they get exactly what they give,
In which they're loved and pampered, not forsaken.

Some waited too long to have a child,
Some to marry, crumple a dull career,
Some to leave a spouse whose voice was mild
But whittled down their soul from year to year.

And some turned wooden in their smiles and tongues
And some paced fragile hour to room to hour
And some took fire and smoke inside their lungs
And turned to powder in their office tower.

Oh, time ticks even in the infant's caul,
On mourners wristwatches despite the Dead.
Somewhere God weeps, sorry for them all.
For what He's written, and for what She's said.

I sometimes see The God in Auschwitz smoke.
For years I watch Him fight internal fires.
At times I heard Her as a dirty joke
Old cronies told maddened by desire

For sex and celebration, holy zest
For golden faith they'd swipe from churches,
Spilling with red wine, Montalcino's best,
For what intrigue can't seize, mere cash can't purchase:

The intimations in the dawning light
That waken in a poet freed from time
Only when passionate, when the mind is right,
Only when stressed, when the soul must scan and rhyme.

YOU

You write about the confines that you feel.
A few friends and relatives read your work.
You see them now and then at readings.
Some say you don't speak loud enough.
Some say you sound rhetorical.
You know Szymborska suffered like you do?
And other poets equal to her
But unknown because they didn't network
Or trade reviews in obscure journals
So they can teach in "major" colleges, not
In towns with one movie theater, three bars,
Roadside shopping malls—strip malls,
Three strip clubs, one Greek diner,

The years of study you spent in universities
Where you had to speak the doublespeak
Of politics, art dressed up as politics.
Once you daydreamed you'd be Yeats,
Eliot, Plath, Lowell, Dylan Thomas.
Shortly you felt anxious, numbed, depressed,
Moreso now, old as you've become,
Retired with a wife you do not love,
With children who do not function,
Waiting for you to die, your wife to die
So they can snatch your scanty savings
From pensions, social security,
Your better furnishings, your mother's jewelry.

Oh, to feel young again, for poetry
To be a major art form again.
Yes, no one starts off without ideals.
Yes, no one continues without deadened hope.

Yes, no one can give up the creative life.
So write then, for your soul's sake
And for your aging tolerant wife.
Please give, without remorse, what you cannot take.

THE STAR

She was voluptuous years ago,
Cast manipulative, charismatic.
Her lines were witty and her cat's smile slow.
In bed she was professionally pneumatic.

The public loved her, though her public's gone.
She wanders in the rooms of her dementia.
She knew her reputation would live on.
She has no memory. She can't venture

Out of her house, out of her single bed.
She squeezes a pillow between her knees.
In lucid moments she wishes she was dead
Or purrs her best line: "Somebody help me, please."

SHAKESPEARE

If I could live a Muslim cabbie's day
Driving in traffic, parking at noon to pray
In 96th Street's mosque, I'd stop to chat
With vendors hawking fruit, pashminas, books
Even about my centuries of fame;
If I could be a New York City hack
I'd give up every sonnet, every play,
Not in disgrace with men's eyes, not in shame
For just one sandwich stuffed with sizzling fat
Plump Falstaff in a greasy apron cooks,
I'd take time, not scripted Fortune, back.

POOLSIDE MOZART

Mozart slips between the fronds
Of every balletic palm,
Fingers each yellow or red
Hibiscus. Sprightly Mozart
Isn't dead. He trills,
Glissandos, double stops
Into the ears of every sun
Bather and nachos muncher
And, like the turquoise water,
Draws the fat, the slim,
The young, the aged in.
Mozart the atmosphere
Swells clouds into arpeggios,
Suspends pelicans on G-strings.
Wigless, powderless, Hispanic
Mozart plays the Caribbean
As he plays Paris, London,
Copenhagen, Prague
Simultaneously.
Mozart digitized
Is mathematics musicalized,
An orderly surprise,
Like this teenaged girl,
Having swallowed too much water,
Spits a perfect cone of spray,
Each drop a solid grace note.

THE WIDOW

She sits in silence, munching her meals.
For company she turns on the TV
Whose presence, like the future, isn't real.
She can't imagine what she doesn't see.

Her closet is as empty as his chair.
She shuffles in his slippers across the floor
And wields his razor to thin out her hair.
But puts the sharp knives in the kitchen drawer.

Despair is in her torso, not her mind.
She has no arms. She has puppet legs.
She holds her head, as if she's ill or blind.
She stares at the phone and pleads, whines, begs.

Her house was loud with hubbub, laughter, talk
Of actions that she can't conceive she took.
She smears cream cheese on a celery stalk
She bites before his mirror, but can't look

At how, despite her will, she's broken down,
At how her ribs are slabs of breathless meat,
At how she fears the clamor of this town,
At how the endless days repeat, repeat.

RESONANCE

Three centuries have passed since she peeled fruit,
Dressed in red and brown and linen white,
Her knife glistening, though it's still and mute.
She sits in silence for Nicolaes Maes.

A napkin on her lap folds in the light
Slipped from a wall, as if light stays.
A skein of skin; a cello's backwards "S"
Waits for its twin, though the knife can't turn.

Her hands hold still, as if they've come to rest
Upon a note a cellist's stopped to coax us,
To keep our eyes, like Maes, simply in focus
On what's to come, but what remains unheard.

IMMORTALITY

Poems are written for the folks at home
Who scoffed at what we said in prose.
Poems are written for the folks who doze
In nursing homes, or villages of stone.

Poems are written for idealized others,
For the best traits in our fathers, mothers.
Poems are transcripts of our chromosomes
That once formed moving flesh and bone.

Poems are written sound by line by page
In momentary grief or fear or age,
Knowing there is no one and no home.
Poems are written for their sake alone.

WHAT HAPPENED

What happened to Mozart who sang like a bird
More golden than Yeats' imagination wrought?
Where is Shakespeare's passionate thought?
Does his ghost pace on Hamlet's stage?
And what of Dante who consigned to Hell
His former friends who did not treat him well?
Where is Sophocles whose simple myth
Became the basis of psychoanalysis
And Freud who smoked his mouth to death,
What happened to him, to his depth
Of soul—is it lying like a clay shard
In an earthen hole, and poor Dylan Thomas
Who ranted, "Death shall have no dominion,"
Knowing he lied, or the Brothers Grimm,
What became of them, dust in sunlight
Turned like a clock—watch it long enough
And you'll go mad, or Paganini
Whose fingers danced and women swooned,
Or Gower, or Chaucer who made
Such exquisite mixes of English and French
The birds that *slepen al with open eye*
Would weep to hear the Earth took him?
What happened to Donne who would have us listen
To sermons about our limitations,
And Boccaccio, a name to stuff in your mouth
As a squirrel stuffs nuts when fall leaves redden?
What of Herbert with his conviction of Heaven
And Apollinaire, that fantastic name,
Verlaine, Villon, Baudelaire, names
That once strode Paris, and Renoir, Cezanne?
What happened to Picasso, where did he go,
And Marc Chagall who would live forever,

And Michelangelo upside down,
Painting all night like a motley clown,
And Jane Austen, so precise about the minutiae
Of interactions, where is her flesh
With its intricate cells,
And Emily Dickinson who lived alone
As if time never happened.
What happened to Einstein,
His brain in a jar,
And Galileo, Copernicus, Blake?
Put them together and what do you make
Of these disappeared, where did they go?
We know but we are too timid to say,
Of Whitman who whistled his own way,
Hands in his pockets, ready to loaf,
Or Frost that dark and folksy man,
Beckett waiting in a garbage can?
All these geniuses and little you
With a pen in your hand, a non-believing Jew,
What of your life, where did it go?
It passed in an instant. Oh.

AGING

"After a while we learn to mourn ourselves."

We talked of aging in the dying light,
And huge ambitions, small accomplishments,
Of hurtful actions, what we really meant.
We stayed up well into the night.

You said, "We're well for now," though nervously,
"9/11 brought this town disease."
"All valleys of death," I joked, "and leafless trees."
You smiled at me dolorously.

Downstairs our block was being lit
For Christmas, strings of light on all the trees,
Snow falling bit by bit by bit.
You kneeled at the window, childlike on your knees.

Did you ever think we would come to this,
We who lived from kiss to kiss to kiss?
Did you think our bodies would frighten us
When we were free and wild and dangerous?

DUSK

After years of tragedy wearing us thin
As butterflies, as delicate and transient,
We find each brownstone brick, each flowerpot
Our eyes alight on, seemingly heaven sent.
And each late hour seems a moment to begin,
A perch defining who we were and who we're not,
Beautiful to each other in our darkening shades,
Dark as these interior walls and balustrades
Where ghosts of Whistler, Sargent, Merritt Chase
Unravel gloves with almost living grace,
Walking toward their future in a distant room
Where butterflies are fixed, cut flowers bloom.

DEPRESSION

I need His thunderous voice, I need The Cross.'
I literally saw devils from my bed
When I was having chemotherapy,
And now I'm scared of aging,
Getting brittle as that wren's bread?

How can you think you just can paint and write,
Fight with your wife, munch that Hershey's, laugh at loss?

Sit with me on this bench in Carl Schurz Park:
It's Mother's Day. See four wrens crowding their nest,
Mom dipping to feed her babies? Life at its best.

"Okay, check your e-mails. Here's one from my friend
Called "The Immortal British Knight,"
Writing, "Now my daughter is in an urn!
Who cares to light a candle in the dark?"
If not in Time we'll piteously burn.

My crowd of doctors call me Job.
"*Three* nearly fatal diseases."
The most painful, though, is this depression
Which does with me what it pleases.

These cherry blossoms are dying fast.
I can't capture them as once I could.
Their shrunken tinges of red can't last.
My brain is twisted as their wood.

If I could write out this depression,
Rid myself of this with a pill,
What use then is my crafty profession,
If I, the doctor, am so ill?

I still help others with their neuroses
Which seem silly next to what I feel:
Dissociated, totally exhausted. God,
These cherry blossoms don't seem real.

THE DOCTOR

Reviewing the century
Decades of which I half-remember
Like thumbing great modernist
Poems, their rhythms
Comfortably familiar,
I stop at Dr. Williams
Who before the war
Which shaped my life
Wrote of pain, plain and simple
In his quotidian town
Where he walked
His house-calls bag
Swinging like a bell,
A stone.

THE MIRACLE OF ORDINARY LIFE

A play of ours that's done, a poem that's read,
A night of making love, a children's park,
A television flickering in the dark,
A boring rainy Sunday afternoon
Are all that differentiate us from the dead
Who tell us both in dreams, "We'll see you soon."
We talk about our memories through the night.
You try to comfort me. I hold you tight
Till one of us falls asleep. The other can't,
Is too afraid to take a sleeping pill.
The other wakes from nightmare in a pant
And says that time is stronger than our will,
We had so many years of being ill.

ORDINARY LIFE

Going from office to home and back
By cab in Spring, Summer, Fall,
Eating in the same two restaurants
Almost every night, without fat, without salt,
Talking about family, about politics
With friends, not friends, reading the news
Papers, sitting at night watching TV
Action movies where people seem animations,
Or typing scripts, or listening to the same
Stories patients tell, or worrying about
Health, seeing doctors week after week,
Or watching sunsets coming earlier,
Doing without skiing, tennis, basketball
Because of injuries, because of pain,
Taking opioids, anti-depressants,
Sleeping pills, feeling numbed
By radiation, chemotherapy,
Hating aging, hating looking in mirrors,
The face on Skype, on Face Time,
Feeling muscles going slack, slacker.

Oh, for being younger, handsome
In years of photographs,
In your country house, in Central Park,
Almost always smiling, satisfied,
Optimistic, adventuresome,
In free Paris, Persia, London, Berlin,
Sun-tanned in cages smacking baseballs
With vigor, with synovial fluid
Between wrist bones, shoulder bones, knee bones,
With no thought of hospitals, mortality.
In an instant you/me could be back there

WANDERING

Younger writer friends talk of retirement,
On teachers' pensions, mutual funds,
Not spend what they've spent lifetimes to save,
Of watching TV movies in the afternoons,
Going to doctors three times a week,
Googling their first loves and jerking off,
Bickering with wives Monday, Tuesday,
Revisiting mistakes that didn't make them famous,
Rich, smugly or not smugly satisfied.
As adolescents they planned to be immortal
Like terrorists—different kinds of martyrs.
Some live for a future where time is stored
For card games, tennis, golf, for vacations
On cruise ships where they'll get fat or on planes
Where they eat peanuts and flirt with stewardesses.
Yet none of these choices matter very much.
Time makes lifetimes ultimately abstract,
Resumes turn into obituaries.
And their grandkids grow like potted plants
And the future is present and the past is past
And their babies will crawl and their babies will walk
And talk and feel safe as they go exploring.
Some of them will stay playwrights,
Martyrs perhaps to self-destruction.
Oh, what remains are the universals,
Nature as Heaven on Earth, Evil
Presenting itself as psychopathology,
The Seven Deadly Sins
In every moment, in every generation.
I wander. I'm catching up with age.

NOT KADDISH

There is comfort in familiarity:
Your health problems, your money problems,
Your wife's body,
Your clothes worn three, four times a week
Since you're broke, broken, soaked
In Time, the unfamiliarity of aging,
Winter coming quicker than leaves falling,
Flowers in your last springs
Withering like your culture dying,
Your body politic dying
As is it has for half a century
In the hypocrisy of The Academy,
The Darkness of American Puritanism

—While in this forever city, this familiar city
Jews, Christians, Muslims, Hindus
Go about their business in rhyme, meter,
Representation, marble sculpture, tonal music,
True scholarship, true religiosity
As if real deaths were not in the streets
Of their original cities, their foreign cities:
Tel Aviv, Mosul, Madrid, Paris
—Original Sin run rampant . . .

So there is comfort in familiarity:
Traffic lights regularly changing,
The summer sun fixed in relative heaven,
Soldiers, cops in uniforms, plain clothes,
Guarding Penn Station, guarding from rooftops
Marathon runners from Brooklyn, Staten Island,
Concert halls, museums, synagogues, churches,
Guarding their familiarity, Death
Momentarily in their custody.

THE FRICK

Overwhelmed by beauty I weep for life
Now that I'm frail, now that I have been sick.
I stroll past Titians, Bellinis with my wife
Into the great long chambers of The Frick

Where huge Turner and Whistlers are lit
As if their lifetimes still exist. Their ships,
Sunsets, gowns, shadows, counterfeit smiles
Bespeak seduction from long vanished lips,

Like Vermeer's Lady who now makes me weep,
As do Rembrandt's characters in theatrical dress,
Even his Polish Rider now long asleep,
And the model for the soldier by Velazquez.

Life, life in Frick's artificial garden,
Where lovers lounge in well-protected planes.
Here Frick at night would wander, stricken
By his daughter's death; only art could keep him sane.

And so his wealth and generous collection
Were like two pockets filled with gold
Coins he could rattle like recollections
Which in his helpless grasp turned simply cold.

THE HOUSE WE HAD TO SELL

This is the house we lived in, white as a bride.
Mozart is echoing the birds outside.
We're sitting at the table playing gin.
My son is laughing every time he wins
Because he's eight, because we're all in love,
Living the future we're still dreaming of.
Spring is in the mountains, green as Oz,
In the fresh-cut flowers in the crystal vase
Mirroring the garden where the bees are thick.
Though everyone was dying, dead or sick,
These were our uncontaminated hours,
Like bottle water sipped by scissored flowers,
Permanent in memory, sealed by the pain
That childhood ends and we can't go home again.

LINES WRITTEN ON A DEDICATED BENCH

The courtyard at Trinity
Church in almost December
Shows pink roses among
Green and red and yellow leaves.
I remember how I sat Then,
My son in my lap
Singing songs he hums to his
Rambunctious two-year-old son.

I won't say where have the years
Gone, not in this forever day
With its church bells ringing,
Its sun constant, its clouds
Permanent, a newspaper
Opened on my lap unread.

All Time exists in this Now,
Among the pink roses.
The long green leaves, the red leaves,
Fallen yellow and brown leaves.

Sh, here a priest with a pure
White collar comes walking slowly,
Contemplating future time
When . . .

DELACORTE'S CLOCK

"Delacorte's chiming. It is sunset."
—*Manhattan Carnival*

My son is my age when I wrote that.
When we were eating crap and smoking still.
Now for the moment we are sunset-fine.
What once was comic now is pluck, luck, will.

Hand in hand we walk toward the chiming clock
And watch the metal animals as we did then
About to move in circles once again.
Except we're tragic and our plot is stock.

Girls in dashikis, hijabs, boys tattoos
Line up for tickets to the park's real zoo.
It's sunny still. The park's September green.
We know that what we're seeing we have seen

In different dialects and different styles.
Delacorte's clock's new melody is off,
Postmodern. We walk under it. You cough.
We plop on a bench, facing a tourist aisle

Where a jazz band: sax, drums, bass
Play *Take Five*, circling with cocaine grace,
We swing dance though we've walked this park for miles.
A gorgeous nun in blue hi-five and smiles,

Then skips away, swinging long worry beads.
She's hooted by two ugly juveniles,
"Fuck me," they laugh. "Fuck *you*," I say. You lead
As the band plays on for quarters, nickels, dimes.

I drop five dollars. "Wow, in these hard times!"
We walk on past an aged children's clown,
A gilded mime determined to survive
This deep recession, this expensive town.

A bum snorts, "Ain't it great to be alive?
We edge away from him to tan our faces.
Two Russian tourists talk like mental cases
On cell phones, with attachments to their ears.

But we'll hear nothing in the coming years!
You take my hand; we squeeze to death our fears.

AS TIME GOES BY

That was a golden age in which we lived.
Each day was summer, God was everywhere,
In every molecule of New York City air
When we were young and just believed in us.
That was a haloed age in which we lived,
Late twentieth summer, love was everywhere.
I'd stop beside you on our walks to stare
At you, buying a peach, climbing a bus's stair.
And there were buts, but always and & and
Sitting in Central, doodling each other's hand,
And I recite poems, my simple fictions
In meter, rhyme, and New York City diction.
As dusk drew near we'd hold a darkening kiss.
When you're distressed, you must remember this.

BIOGRAPHICAL NOTE

Frederick Feirstein has had nine previous books of poems published, seven by Story Line and the Quarterly Review of Literature. He has been the recipient of a Guggenheim Fellowship, the Poetry Society of America's John Masefield Award, and England's Arvon Prize. Twelve of his plays have been produced. Three are musical dramas, his lyrics deriving from his poetry. His third, *Uprising*, will be done as a film. He made his living writing film and television while he trained as a psychoanalyst. He is in private practice in New York City and on the faculty of the National Psychological Association for Psychoanalysis. His autobiography is in the Contemporary Authors Autobiography Series and his biography in the Dictionary of Literary Biography.